121
Seven-Word Poems

JEF HARRIS

JHP Publishing Bel Air

Copyright © 2022 by Jef Harris
All rights reserved. No part of this book may be reproduced or used in any manner without the written permission of the copyright owner except for the use of quotations in a book review. For more information, address: jef@jefharrispoems.com

First paperback edition March 2023

Cover Illustrations by Ayan Mansoori

ISBN 978-1-7357154-1-4 (paperback)

www.jefharrispoems.com

Some of these poems first appeared on Jef Harris Poems Facebook page between October 2015 and April 2019

About this Book

This project began as a writing experiment for Jef Harris Poems' Facebook page in October 2015. Jef Harris sought to create micro poems, with as few words as possible, that substantiated realities in his life circumstances. Seven words were the lowest applicable number chosen to present his cognition. Stretching poetic conventions to the edge of making sense, omitting verbs and articles without burying ideas, thoughts, or interpretation. He also sampled numbers of words below seven. However, seven words are ideal for the ideas presented in this project. Therefore,

1
Read each line as an individual poem.

Contents

About God..4

Others..8

On Poetry..14

For Fun..17

For Foodies...21

Some Poems About Me...........................23

A Few Blessings......................................29

About the Author....................................32

ABOUT GOD

2

First thing first, give thanks to God!

3

For they that love God, hear Him.

4

Hate the seven things the Lord hates.

5

Let me tell you about God's love.

6

Love is not arrogant; hatred is haughty!

7

Love magnifies God, not the human being.

8

Love rejoices whenever truth wins over injustices.

Seven-Word Poems

9
Rest! Let your heart not be troubled.

10
Say the Name that's above all names!

11
They that know God will see Him.

12
The magic of love is its divinity.

13
Wearing God's armor has never been tiresome.

14
All of His magnificent works are perfect.

15
Sing when He pours His glory out!

16
The magic of divinity? God is love!

121
Seven-Word Poems

OTHERS

17
Avoid loud, abrasive people: they will wound.

18
Calling all sensible minds—rethink our society!

19
Can you speak to me without talking?

20
Conservative strategists do know what is best.

21
Evaluate audiences to avoid preaching to choirs.

22
First, see me without using your eyes.

23
He provided seamless transitions to pathetic disinformation.

24
I thought I forgot about you…crap!

25
Your artistic innovations grazed me once more.

26
I'm not what you think you need!

27
If not through you, through who then?

28
Kiss me again without using your lips!

29
Malcontent, misguided, malicious, manipulating, maltreatment-manufacturing Marxist!

30
New eligibility requirement: Candidates cannot be mindless.

31
Nihilistic, nasty, narcissistic, narrow-minded, naive nincompoop!

32
O, the anguish of COVID-19 bereaved persons!

33
Oppressive, opulent, obstinate, oblivious, obnoxious, old oligarch!

34
Play me a reel, cute ginger fiddler!

35
Pretentious, presumptuous, pudgy, phallic, prideful, prevaricating pedophile.

36
She generates volumes of hot air daily!

37
Sing me an Advent hymn, Korean girl!

38
Sing me another patriotic song, conservative millennial!

39
Sing me that easy isicathamiya, dark man.

40
I'm studying the public…eating an Enchilada.

41
Tell me what you've done by faith.

42
The nicest thing you've ever done: lived!

43
You're never too repugnant for His Son.

44
Where are you? My heart's still broken!

45
What experiential learning did you gain today?

46
Take steps not to become a soft target.

47
Sing me another consecration hymn, bright beauty!

On Poetry

48
Poetry's not the same as food labels.

49
I can't stomach lame arguments against poetry.

50
I'm going to nurture another poem now.

51
Usually, I despise writing about my illnesses.

52
Please, no reading poems like reading newspapers!

53
Perfecting virtuous patience is an advanced art!

54
This poem feeds readers words that dance.

55
These are poems that promote linear thinking.

56
Valiant men give birth to healthy poems.

57
Mother of all poems: Psalm twenty-three.

For Fun

58
I assisted in this for the food.

59
I despise writer's block because, uh, hmm?

60
Who's endured hours of interrogations by preteens?

61
Daily, I take time for short intermissions.

62
I confess: I have lied to telemarketers.

63
I support the Mad Koala Liberation Front!

64
I'm addicted to estrogen—no help required.

65
Precrastination is a thing; I'm doing it!

66
If silence is golden, is noise rusty?

67
Indebted? Not to one of you nerds!

68
O, the thrill of making yellow lights!

69
Do dark, jagged scars count as tattoos?

70
That last rant came out like spew!

71
Tonight, I'm roasting some medium-well insomnia.

72
Where the heck is my Slide Rule?

For Foodies

73
Don't eat the black spots on Cauliflower!

74
No apology; I only eat goat cheese.

75
The bomb: A Cuban sandwich on rye!

76
When Mirepoix goes foul, blame the carrots!

77
Yum: Caviar, foie gras, crackers...Kool-Aid!

78
What wine pairs with ancho-peppered walnuts?

Some Poems About Me

Seven-Word Poems

79
All of my poems are my daughters.

80
Arguments about religion make me sick too!

81
Even my shadow is releasing endorphins today!

82
For seventy years, my "Yes" meant "Yes."

83
I am always learning how to forgive!

84
I break through writer's block with music.

85
I can't stomach any arguments about politics.

86
I dance on injustices and fake news.

87
I misled my wicked adversary's decision-makers.

88
I did it for King and Country!

89
I ignite when my morals get jeopardized.

90
I love people seeing Christ in me!

91
I now know the gravity of love.

92
I only have one woman to please!

93
I overcame many addictions through Christ alone.

94
I survived the brink of destruction again!

95
The evilest thief I know is time.

96
I'm conjuring the patience of leap years.

97
I'm not a son of the world!

98
I'm always collecting data on my weaknesses.

99
I'm coping in a mad, viral world!

100
I've never played dead to stay alive.

101
If not for grace, I'd be mad!

102
My boyhood thoughts weren't always about girls.

103
No apology; I don't believe in recycling!

104
O, my dreams of warm African winds!

105
I am conjuring the courage of Christ!

106
Yes, I want to sing Spanish lullabies.

107
I know how to walk by faith.

108
When I say, "I love," I love!

109
"Bear me safe above, a ransomed soul." (This one is in the Public Domain)

A Few Blessings

110
God bless those who have known desolation.

111
May divine favor surround you like air!

112
May the weight of your grief decrease.

113
May you learn to trust God alone.

114
May you learn what wisdom truly is.

115
May your scales of rejection fall away.

116
Blessed are the souls that stand guard.

117
May you have the mind of Christ.

118
May you get wisdom before all else!

119
May your pain end with His name!

120
May you live like you are loved.

121
God bless all souls with broken hearts.

About the Author

Jef Harris began writing lyric poetry in 1960s Chicago. He developed this style into songwriting. "Each song begins with a poem or a prayer," he said. He published in *World of Poetry Press, New York Poetry Foundation Anthology, American Poetry Anthology,* the Haiku anthology *In this House: If Walls Could Talk,* and other publications in Germany and America. His debut collection, *First Poem of Words*, published in 2012.

www.ingramcontent.com/pod-product-compliance
Lightning Source LLC
Chambersburg PA
CBHW030047100526
44590CB00011B/349